Sacred: Stopping

The Six Keys to Returning to Your True Self

"You don't become someone new. You become someone true."

Disclaimer & Mission Statement

● I am not a psychiatrist, doctor, or therapist. I do not offer medical or psychological counseling. I am not a guru, shaman, or philosopher. My work is not about titles or doctrines—it is about awareness, action, and personal responsibility.

If you need professional medical, psychological, or therapeutic support, I strongly encourage you to seek help from qualified professionals in those fields.

TABLE OF CONTENTS

Dedication

To my parents and my brother

My mother, whose heart was both soft and strong, met life's challenges with grace. Raising five children, including one with Down syndrome, she never once complained. With dignity, devotion, and a spirit that never wavered, she created a home filled with care, resilience, and love. Her influence endures in the strength and compassion she planted within us.

My father, whose presence I carry still, grew up in hard times and became a man whose word was his bond. Loyal, honest, and steadfast, he lived with quiet strength and unwavering integrity. What he believed, he lived. And what he lived, he passed on: a person is only as good as his word.

And my little brother, who lived with Down syndrome and revealed to me more about unconditional love and quiet strength than any classroom ever could. He found joy in simple things, especially watching The Andy Griffith Show, where Sheriff Andy was his hero. In time, his dream was honored when Mt. Sterling, Kentucky, sheriff department recognized him as an honorary sheriff — his picture proudly placed in the newspaper. His life was a reminder that dignity, love, and courage are not measured by circumstance, but by the heart.

To my beautiful children

To Susan, Clyde, Melissa— You have been part of this journey since the very beginning. Susan, you were in the background cheering me on. Melissa, you just graduated high school. Clyde, you were preparing to be deployed overseas. I still remember the day you asked me, "Dad, why is it taking God so long to answer you?" Looking back, I now understand when we have been deeply conditioned, it takes time to unravel the words and beliefs that once shaped us. It takes patience, focus, and the courage to think critically, seek evidence, and face ourselves with honesty.

Thank you for walking with me through that process— for your love, questions, and your presence. This book holds the gold nuggets I discovered along the way.

Savannah

Thank you for your steady support throughout my journey, and for the creative legacy you have brought into the world through your own writing. Though our paths have taken different directions, your encouragement and presence in those foundational years remain deeply appreciated

With Gratitude

To the friends I met along the way—some as clients, others as new acquaintances —you became something more.

To Dr. John Paul Broderson and Paul Jr.— friends disguised as clients. Thank you for your kindness, the deep conversations, quality cigars, and some fine bourbon, along with both unshakable wisdom.

To Chaplain Gerard Howell —Our friendship began at a turning point in my life, and your trust opened the door for me to share a message of hope within the Fayette County Detention Center. From our first conversation to the many meals shared with you and Jane, your life and leadership left a lasting mark.

To Dr. Marylee James —a powerful spirit and a deep soul. You showed me what truth looks like on the other side of pain. Our many conversations were open, honest, and clear. Your presence and wisdom is felt deeply.

To Ronald E. Butler — writer, attorney, and encourager. Thank you for staying in my corner and believing in this work before it had a name.

To Jim McDonald — You treated me like a man before I knew how to be one. You saw something in me — and I have never forgotten.

To Dan Jackson—Thank you for your friendship, thoughtful guidance, and generous insight throughout this journey. Your contributions helped share this book in ways that brought greater clarity, structure, and depth. I am grateful for the path we have shared and the meaningful influence you continue to have—both in my life and in the lives of many.

To Annette Hamm —an accountability partner, coach, and steady encourager. Your presence helped me stay focused and finish this book. We first met through Jack Canfield's program, and since then your insight, discipline, and support have been a gift. I am grateful for the suggestions for the book and the clarity you bring and the friendship we share.

To All of You — From the moment we met, there was an undeniable connection. Thank you for the gift of your presence and the light you brought to this world. Your service to humanity does not go unnoticed.

About the Author

Art Tincher was born in Louisville, Kentucky and raised in the quiet rhythm of farm life where work began early, nature spoke often, and nothing was wasted. By the age of 12, he was working. By the time he was grown, he had seen enough to know that life doesn't always move in straight lines, but it always leaves signs.

Artt has spent his life walking between worlds from the fields to the pulpit, from religious duty to spiritual awakening.

His journey through ministry opened him to deeper questions about what it means to be human, to suffer, to search, and to find. What he found wasn't more dogma — but a quieter voice within. That's when he awakened to this reality: Sacred Stopping.

Today, Artt teaches the sacred art of slowing down of stopping, listening, and returning to what's already true inside. He believes meditation isn't an escape from reality but the key to re-entering it awake.

Sacred Pause

Breath—*Gives **life.***

Presence—*Is **pure.***

Awareness—*Speaks with **clarity.***

Preface

I have written this for those who are in transition: a new career, healthier relationships, a deeper understanding of your identity, an undated belief or a more fulfilled life with a purpose that lights your passion.

If you are thinking about change, feeling it, or needing it. This book is for you. It is written, with space to breathe.

This is not just a book. It is a reflection—an invitation to reconnect with yourself, your breath, your awareness, and your inner guidance.

You won't find quick fixes or productivity hacks in these pages. What you will find is space—space to pause, reflect, and reset. Space that has been missing in a world too focused on speed, noise, and external conditioning.

Many of the words in this book—stop, listen, presence, breath, stillness—are more than ideas.

They are practical tools. Some will speak to your logic. Others will speak to something deeper—something you've felt but haven't always put into words. Both are welcome. Let the physical and spiritual parts of you find unity in this experience.

Stopping: A Personal Turning Point

After spending over 20 years deeply invested in ministry—guiding others, leading with purpose, and practicing devotion—I began to feel a shift in late 2002. At the time, I had just bought a new home for my family, a place that symbolized provision, progress, and gratitude. My wife at the time had poured her heart into making that vision possible. It felt like everything should have been settled and complete.

But something within me was stirring. The change I felt wasn't loud—it was subtle. It wasn't what I expected change to look like. I had thought it would come in the form of external success or divine affirmation. Instead, it came through a deep inner questioning, a quiet discomfort, and an unexplainable pull toward something more.

Then, in early 2003, I made a decision to stop. To listen deeply—I went inward. What followed was five hours of intentional silence that would alter the course of my life forever.

In that silence, I didn't find a distant deity. I found a deep awareness within myself.
It wasn't a voice from above—it was a knowing from within.

That moment of awakening revealed something profound:
The presence I had searched for was never separate.
It was awareness itself—consciousness, clarity, unlimited—
potential.

I began to see how the systems I once trusted had often shaped belief through fear and control. But presence—true presence—freed me. It showed me that real transformation doesn't come through performance or perfection. It comes through stillness, honesty, and the willingness to let go.

That's why I wrote this book.
To invite you to stop.
To listen.
And to return to what has always been inside you.

There is a part of you that already knows.
It's been waiting—not for more effort, but for a moment of stillness.
To hear the answers you need now, it's in the silence in which truth is revealed.

If you are contemplating change—if life is stirring something inside you that feels unfamiliar—know this:

You are being called inward.

Like an acorn holding the blueprint of a mighty oak, your unlimited potential is —waiting.

But potential can't grow while sitting on a shelf. It needs the right conditions—time, stillness, presence, and nourishment.

And when the outer shell begins to soften, what's been hidden can finally emerge.

Awakening.
Presence.
Becoming the new, true you.

How to Read This Book with Intention

• Slow Down – This book is not meant to be rushed. Pause when something resonates. Let it breathe.

• Let the Words Work – Familiar words may be used in new ways. Let them speak to both your mind and your deeper awareness. Glossary provided on Page: 117

• Use the Reflections – Each chapter includes questions and a mantra. Don't skip them. They turn insight into practice.

• Breathe as You Read – Notice your breath. Let it slow you down. Let it ground you.

• Make It Practical – This book is not here to impress. It is here to help you notice patterns and act from inner clarity.

• Return as Needed – You don't need to read it straight through. Take your time.

And remember this:

Stopping is the invitation. Stopping is choosing.

It is the sacred reset that brings you back to who you were designed to be.
In a noisy world, stopping allows clarity to rise, fear to fade, and identity to re-emerge.

This book is not here to replace your truth.
It's here to point you to return to it.

Stop. Listen. Learn. Apply. Develop. Become.
This is a path. This is the awakening— This is a pure moment.

The Four Pillars of Fulfillment

Before we begin Chapter 1, It's important to understand the deeper foundation that supports everything in this book.
At the core of our transformation are four essential human drives. When these are met, we feel aligned, awake, and whole. When they're neglected, we can feel disconnected, fragmented, confused, or lost.

The Four Pillars of Fulfillment

Identity
Who am I?
(Self-awareness, roles, internal coherence)

Purpose
Why do I do what I do?
(Direction, meaning, motivation)

Passion
What makes me come alive?
(Creativity, joy, energy)

Contribution
What am I giving back?
(Connection, service, legacy)

Understanding the Four Pillars—Identity, Purpose, Passion, and Contribution—gives us clarity on what we truly seek. But how do we get there?

 In a world that constantly pulls our attention outward, the journey inward is both sacred and essential.

This book offers that connection.

Identity

Who am I?

Reconnecting with who you are beneath the roles, routines, and responsibilities. This is your essence—not just what you do, but who you are when everything else is quiet.

Purpose

Why am I here?

The guiding thread that gives direction and meaning to your life. Purpose is the deeper reason behind your daily decisions. When you live on purpose, you're no longer drifting. You're choosing, where you spend your time, attention and what you focus on.

Passion

What makes me come alive?

Passion fuels your energy and inspiration. It's what brings joy, excitement, and creativity into your life. This pillar reminds us that life isn't just about living —it's about feeling what you are living. Logically and emotionally connected.

Contribution

What am I giving to the world?

Fulfillment isn't complete until what's within you flows outward. This pillar is about service, impact, and legacy. When you give from wholeness, you live with a deeper meaning.

The Sacred Six: How We Return to Ourselves

Through six conscious movements—Stop, Listen, Learn, Apply, Develop, Become—you are invited to walk a path that reclaims your true identity. Each step is simple, but not shallow. Each one builds upon the last, guiding you.

STOP → Reconnect with Identity

Stopping is the first revolution. It breaks the trance of busyness. You stop running. Stop escaping. Stop reacting. You pause long enough to see—not just the world around you, but the one within you.
In that stillness, identity starts to rise. You begin to remember who you are beneath the noise.

LISTEN → Clarify Purpose

Once you stop, you can finally hear—not the chaos of the world, but the quiet awareness inside you. The wisdom and the knowing. Listening helps you ask: Why am I here? What am I truly here to do—not just to survive, but to serve something greater? No matter what part of the journey you are on these questions can be revisit. I highly recommend checking in with yourself at various times. We are always evolving.

LEARN → Awaken Passion

True learning is not memorizing facts—it's remembering truth. It's when something resonates so deeply you feel your whole being say yes. Learning with awareness awakens your passion—your natural curiosity, joy, and inspiration.

APPLY → Live with Integrity

Knowledge without action is just noise. When you apply what you've learned, you begin to live in alignment. You don't just talk about your values—you embody them. This is how passion becomes expression, and insight becomes impact.

DEVELOP → Strengthen Contribution

As you apply, you develop—not just skills, but strength, character, consistency, and compassion. You realize you have something more to offer—not just to yourself, but to others. You develop not to be perfect, but to be present, passionate, and ready to give yourself to the mission.

BECOME → Fulfill Your Human Design

Becoming is not a destination—it's a return.
You become who you've always been beneath the conditioning.
You become aware, alive, and aligned.
You don't just become someone new—you become fully, deeply you.

This is the vision of real transformation. These are not steps to rush through—they are sacred movements to lean-into.
Each one is a pure moment, a mirror, a reconnection. Together, they open the door to fulfillment—not as a distant dream, but as a lived experience.

There is a deeper intelligence within each of us—beyond the noise, beyond the roles, beyond the survival.
It exists in what many call the Zero Point Field—a space of pure awareness, pure potential, and pure design.

This intelligence knows who you are. It knows why you're here.
It's not trying to control your life—it's trying to express through it.

The six sacred movements in this book are not teachings to memorize.

They are invitations to return to that field—to the original wisdom within you—so it can be lived, embodied, and made real in human form.

Remember: Breath. Presence. Awareness.

Enjoy – Art Tincher

Meditation Reflection

*Take a **moment** to honor your breath.*

*The **first** one brought you here.*

*The last one will carry you **home**.*

***What** you do with the ones in between—**that is your choice**.*

Chapter One: Stop

"Almost everything will work again if you unplug it for a few minutes... including you."

Anne Lamott

The Problem

We live in a time where stopping feels illegal. Slowing down is seen as a weakness. Stillness is mistaken for laziness. We brag about being busy — like exhaustion is a badge of honor. And yet, we can be disconnected from our real purpose in life. Behind the curated photos and filtered smiles, many are unhappy. Sleep-deprived. Spiritually dry. Mentally scattered. Emotionally burnt out.

It's not because we're weak. It's because we're being conditioned — constantly — to stay in motion. Keep pushing. Keep checking. Keep responding. Keep consuming. Keep producing. We've become so used to this frantic rhythm that we don't even notice how unnatural it is. Constant motion has become the baseline. Stillness feels like failure, Why? Because we are now living in the matrix.

But let's get real. How's that working out?

We've created a society of stimulation junkies. We wake up to screens. We eat while scrolling. We work while distracted. We rest by binging. Every moment is filled. Every silence is avoided.

And even when we're alone, we're never truly alone — because we're always plugged in.

This isn't productivity. It's spiritual malnourishment. We are starving in a land of noise.

And the worst part? We don't even know it. We think this is just how life is, that this disconnection — from ourselves, from nature, from each other — is just a side effect of modern life. It's not.

It's a illusion... A psychic fracture.

And the cure begins with one radical move:

Stop.

Not pause. Not slow down. Stop.

That means no screen. No scroll. No distractions. Just you — sitting, breathing, being — with whatever comes up. That space you keep avoiding. That's where the answers live. That's where the real awakening begins. But you'll never reach it if you're too busy to be still.

The Conditioning
So how did we get here? You weren't born distracted. You were trained to be. Every app you use, every platform you visit, every notification you get — it's all designed to pull your focus and keep it.

There are entire industries profiting off your attention. And they are exceptionally good at it.

They've studied how to hook your brain. They know your dopamine triggers. They've gamified your feed, your inbox, your news,

Your notifications. You've been psychologically programmed to stay addicted to distraction.

We don't check our phones anymore — we live in them.

We've learned to panic when we're unreachable. To fear missing out. To crave constant stimulation. We treat boredom like a disease when it's actually a doorway.

And it's not just the phone. It's your schedule. Your obligations. Your addiction to "productivity." You've been conditioned to associate stillness with failure. To feel guilty when you rest. To measure your worth by how much you produce, how fast you move, and how much you can handle.

But you're not a machine.

You're a human being with a nervous system, a soul, a need for quietness.

This endless doing is not sustainable. The burnout isn't just physical — it's spiritual. It's psychic. We've become people who cannot sit alone with ourselves without grabbing something to distract us. And that's not okay.

Because if you can't sit with yourself, you can't know yourself.

And if you don't know yourself, you'll believe whatever the world tells you.

That you're not enough. That you're behind. That you need to buy something, fix something, hustle more, do more, be more.

But here's the truth:

You don't need more.

You need to stop.

The Psychic Cost

When you never stop, you lose more than energy. You lose your inner compass.

You start to forget what your own voice sounds like. You lose touch with your intuition. Your nervous system stays stuck on high alert, flooded with cortisol, exhausted but wired. And even though you're constantly consuming — information, media, opinions — you're not actually digesting it, You're just absorbing, reacting, absorbing, reacting.

This doesn't just scatter your attention. It splits your identity.

You start to operate in fragments. One part of you is posting. Another part is pretending. Another is panicking. You're never fully here. Never fully anywhere. You're just hovering — half-present in every moment, trying to keep up, trying not to drown in the digital tide.

And when you live like that long enough, something happens:

You become psychically fragmented.

Your sense of self gets diluted by noise. Your soul becomes background static. You start living in your head — bouncing between tasks, screens, and anxieties — while your body goes numb and your heart grows quiet. You become a shell with a to-do list.

And then the symptoms show up.

Insomnia. Brain fog. Anxiety. Depression. Irritability. Numbness. Exhaustion. That ache you can't name. That feeling of being constantly behind. That low-level dread that never fully leaves.

We normalize this because most people around us are going through the same thing. But that doesn't make it normal. This isn't life. This is survival mode on repeat. This is the cost of never stopping.

And let's talk about the bigger picture. Because this isn't just personal — it's planetary.

A society that can't stop is a society that can't think clearly. Can't connect. Can't feel. Can't grow. When people are too distracted to go inward, they become easy to manipulate. They become reactive, tribal, and emotionally volatile. They stop asking big questions. They stop imagining new futures. They stop evolving.

This is why stillness is not a luxury — it's a revolutionary act.

To unplug is to reclaim your power.

To stop is to break the trance.

To be quiet is to remember who you are — and what you are not.

You are not a product. You are not a profile. You are not a brand or, a click or a cog. You are a human being with depth, with soul, with wisdom that lives beneath the surface — and the only way to reach it is to stop long enough to hear it.

But nobody's going to hand that space to you. The machine wants your attention. It feeds on your distraction. It thrives on your exhaustion.

So you have to make a choice.

You can keep scrolling, keep running, keep reacting — and keep fracturing.

Or you can stop.

You can sit in the discomfort. You can face the silence. You can reclaim your presence, inch by inch.

And when you do, you'll start to notice something strange:

You come back.

Your energy starts to rebuild.

Your thoughts slow down.

Your breath deepens.

The noise fades.

And there you are — the real you — right beneath the static.

You've been there the whole time.

The Power of Stillness

Stillness isn't just the absence of noise. It's the presence of something deeper.

When you stop — really stop — something happens. At first, it's uncomfortable. The mind doesn't know what to do with silence. You'll feel the itch to check something. The pull to get up, to do, to move. That's withdrawal. That's detox. Let it pass.

Stay still, anyway.

Because beneath the noise, beneath the constant scroll and endless stimulation, there's a part of you that's been waiting for stillness like it's oxygen. A part that doesn't speak in alerts or headlines. A part that remembers who you were before the world told you who to be.

That part of you lives in stillness.

Stillness is where truth shows up. Not the kind of truth that's argued about online — but the kind that sits quietly in your heart. It's the kind of knowing that doesn't need to be proven or posted. It just is.

Stillness is where your body recalibrates. Your nervous system unwinds. Your breathing slows. Your heart rate evens out. You come out of fight-or-flight and into presence. Your cells start to recover. Your energy starts to return.

Stillness is where your mind clears. The mental fog lifts. You see what's yours to carry — and what was never yours in the first place. The looping thoughts begin to settle. And suddenly, the space you feared — the silence — becomes spacious.

Ideas show up there. Insights. Creativity. Vision.

Stillness is not passive. It's powerful. It's alive. It listens. It reveals. It heals.

And maybe most importantly — stillness is the only place where you can feel the unified field of consciousness. Not conceptually. Directly.

Because here's the truth that nobody told us: your mind isn't supposed to be split in two all the time. Left brain calculating. Right brain reacting. Logic battling emotion. Task lists warring with imagination. That division keeps you fragmented.

But stillness unifies.

It's where the hemispheres sync. Where the mental noise drops low enough for the soul to speak. Where you stop performing and start being. Where you don't need to prove anything, chase anything, fix anything — because for the first time in a long time, you remember:

You're already whole.

That wholeness isn't something you earn. It's something you remember. And you can't remember it in chaos. You can't access it through noise. You only find it when you stop long enough to return to yourself.

The world will not encourage this.

You won't get a notification telling you to go within. You have to create that space for yourself. You have to protect it like your life depends on it — because, in many ways, it does.

This stillness? It's not a weakness. It's your reset button.

It's where you begin again — not as a scattered product of your environment, but as a conscious, whole, aware human being.

Stillness is how you remember that you are not on your schedule.

You are not your screen time.

You are not your stress.

You are not your speed.

The Call to Stop
Let's stop pretending this is fine.

Let's stop pretending that being burnt out, overwhelmed, overstimulated, and always-on is just "how life is now." Let's stop numbing ourselves with noise. Let's stop measuring our worth by how many tasks we check off while silently needing stillness.

You don't need another hack, another app, another routine, another productivity tip.

You need to stop.

Stop running from your own presence.

Stop filling every second with stimulation.

Stop treating silence like it's dangerous.

Because silence is sacred, stillness is pure. And you've been trained to treat both like a threat — not because they're dangerous, but because they're powerful.

Because stillness doesn't let you hide.

It brings everything up. The truth. The pain. The things you've buried under distraction. But here's the thing: you need to see those things. You need to face them. You need to feel them — not to suffer, but to release, to heal, to grow.

And you can't do that if you're constantly running from moment to moment, alert to alert, dopamine hit to dopamine hit.

Stopping is the beginning of remembering.

Remembering who you are beneath the chaos. Remembering what actually matters. Remembering that you were never meant to live like this — fractured, reactive, always chasing the next thing.

You were meant to live fully.

With presence. With clarity. With direction that comes from within.

But that requires space. It requires silence. It requires the strength to say:

"I'm unplugging now."

Not forever. Not dramatically. Just long enough to feel yourself again. Long enough to breathe. Long enough to remember that you're not here to survive your schedule — you're here to be alive.

You want to change your life?

You want clarity? transparency, vision? peace?

Then, shut the noise off.

Sit down.

And stop.

Do it awkwardly. Do it imperfectly. Do it even when it feels pointless. Just start.

Because you cannot build a whole life on a fractured foundation, you can't fake your way into fulfillment. You can't outsource awareness.

You have to be willing to sit in the stillness long enough to become who you were meant to be.

That's where it begins.

Right here. Right now. Just stop.

Reflection: Space

*Each section is an invitation to **pause, reflect**, and **return** — not who you were told to be, but who you already are underneath the **noise**.*

May this space become your **mirror**.

REFLECT: *Stop. Take a **moment** and write **what is on your mind.** You will be glad you did. When you finish the last chapter, come back and look at what you were **thinking.***

REFLECT: *What am **I avoiding** by staying busy?*

REFLECT: *What truth always finds me when I am **still**?*

A *Mantra* Gives Voice to Your Intention

*A mantra **is** simply a phrase that helps you come back to the **present** moment —*

*a gentle **anchor** for the mind.*

Let it be soft.

Let it be steady.

*Let it **guide** you home.*

*In stopping, I **return**.*

Sacred Pause

Breath—*I am* **alive.**

Presence—*I am* **here.**

Awareness— *Speak to* **me.**

7-Minute Meditation to a True You

You are already in your quiet space — you've arrived.

Before beginning, set your timer for the seven-minute meditation.

As you read these words, experience them.

Let the practice meet you right here.

Take a slow breath in through your nose,

Exhale gently, let your shoulders drop releasing any stress.

Breathe and follow the natural rhythm. Feel the freshness in the air.

Follow the breath as it enters and leaves your body.

Just be here.

There is nothing you need to fix.

There is nothing you need to do.

Value this moment — it is pure.

Simply be here — with your breath, your mind, and your body.

This is pure presence.

Now, bring your attention to your heart.

Place your right hand gently over your heart — your identity, purpose, passion, and contribution live here.

"Pause for a moment"

"Just Breathe… and listen to your true self" — it already knows the way."

Now remember — you are not what has happened to you.

You choose to move forward from this pure place.

New decisions.

New hope.

New beginnings.

Breathe that in —

and let it guide you forward.

Say silently or aloud:

"I have returned to this moment.

I am at peace.

I am complete.

I am at home."

When you are ready, carry this pure moment into your day.

I encourage you to return to this practice for the next seven consecutive days.

If this is your first time, celebrate it—each beginning matters.

And when this chapter has settled into your life, I'd be grateful if you shared a review. Your experience may guide someone else home to themselves.

Chapter Two: Listen

"The beginning of wisdom is the silence of the tongue."

Democritus

Noise vs. Signal
You've stopped. You've unplugged. You've made space.
Now comes the next step: listen.

But here's the hard truth — most of what we call "listening" isn't real listening. It's mental noise bouncing off the walls of our inner echo chamber. It's not clarity. It's clutter.

We don't hear reality — we hear our programming.

From the moment we wake up, we're hit with noise: headlines, messages, alerts, opinions, ads, fears, shame, judgment, demands. Our brains are trained to absorb it all, recycle it, and spit it back out in loops. And then we mistake that loop for thought. For truth. For identity.

It's not.

It's just noise.

Noise tells you to panic.
Noise tells you you're not enough.
Noise tells you to rush, to fear, to compare, to consume.

Signal is different.

Signal is quiet.
Signal is simple.
Signal doesn't shout — it speaks.

But you can't hear it until you learn to tell the difference.

Noise is anxious. Signal is calm.
Noise is urgent. Signal is grounded.
Noise changes every day. Signal stays the same.

Noise is the voice of the world trying to own your attention.
Signal is the voice of truth — the part of you that's always been
there, quietly waiting for you to listen.

To hear the signal, you have to tune your awareness like a dial. You
have to turn the volume down on everything else. That's why
stopping was so important — it gave you back control of your
frequency. Now, you get to decide what you're tuned into.

This is the beginning of deep listening — not just with your ears, but
with your whole being.

Because the truth is, the most important messages of your life won't
come through a screen. They won't come from someone else's
mouth. They'll come from within.

And if you never learn to listen, you'll miss them.

You'll miss the cue to change.

You'll miss the insight that could unlock the next level of your life.

You'll miss the signal that tells you this isn't for me, or this is what I'm here to do.

And you'll keep mistaking the noise for direction.

But here's the shift:

You can train yourself to hear the signal again.

It starts by asking:

- Is this thought mine?
- Is this emotion new, or is it recycled?
- Is this voice helping me or keeping me trapped?

That kind of awareness — that kind of listening — begins to cut through the static. And that's when things start to change. Because once you hear the signal, you can follow it. And when you follow it, you stop living by default and start living by design.

What Are You Listening To?
Your inner world is not a monologue. It's a whole crowd.

And not everyone in that crowd is telling the truth.

Some voices in your head are echoes. Old programming. Parental expectations. Cultural conditioning. Trauma loops. Survival instincts. Outdated beliefs. Fear dressed up as logic. Shame pretending to be disciplined. They speak loudly. They speak first. They speak often.

But they are not your soul.

Your soul is not panicked. It's not harsh. It doesn't attack you when you fall short. It doesn't whisper, "You're behind," or "You're not enough," or "You'll never change." That's the voice of conditioning — the voice of everything you picked up from the outside and started repeating on the inside.

"Listening deeply means learning to sort the voices"

Ask yourself:

- Who taught me this voice?
- Does this voice bring clarity or confusion?
- Would I speak to someone I love the way this voice speaks to me?

You'll be surprised how much of your internal dialogue isn't even yours.

You absorbed it. You inherited it. You practiced it. And now it sounds like you — but it's not. It's a voice that was useful once, maybe even necessary for survival. But now? Now, it's keeping you trapped.

The real you — the voice of your inner wisdom, your deeper self — speaks differently.

It speaks in a tone that's calm even when firm.
It speaks in direction, not shame.
It speaks in alignment, not urgency.
It speaks in resonance. It says things that make your chest expand instead of contract.

But here's the thing: that voice won't compete for your attention. It won't scream over the chaos. It waits for quietness. It waits for you to get still enough to recognize it.

And when you start to listen to it — really listen — you notice something powerful:

It was always there.

It's the voice that told you; this job isn't it.
The voice that whispered, You're tired — rest.
The one that pulled you toward something more honest.
The one that said let it go before you knew why.
The one that urged you to leave, to stay, to speak, to stay silent —
even when it made no logical sense.

That's not self-doubt. That's not fear. That's signal.

And when you start following that voice instead of the noise, your life changes direction. You start living in alignment, not reaction. You stop waiting for permission. You stop outsourcing your knowing.

Because listening isn't just about hearing more.

It's about hearing right.

The Language of the Body
Your body doesn't lie.

Long before your mind catches up, your body is already speaking. It tells you when something's off. It tightens. It tenses. It pulls away. It slumps. It clenches. And when something's right? It opens. It relaxes. It expands. It leans in.

But here's the issue: most people don't speak their body's language. They override it. Numb it. Distrust it.

We've been conditioned to treat the body like a machine — something to be controlled, optimized, pushed, and ignored until it breaks. We were taught to think our way through life, not feel our way through it.

But the truth is, the body knows first.

Before the thought. Before the story. Before the rationalization. Your body is already signaling you. And if you don't know how to listen, you'll miss critical information.

- That stomach drop when something's wrong. Signal.
- That rush of calm around the right person. Signal.
- That fatigue that hits when you're pretending. Signal.
- That tight chest when you're betraying yourself. Signal.

These aren't random sensations. They're intelligence. They're your nervous system, your gut, your heart, your spirit — trying to get your attention. But most people are so disconnected they don't notice until it turns into sickness. Until the tension becomes chronic. The burnout becomes unbearable. The body finally says: I can't keep holding this for you.

So listening means tuning in — not just mentally, but physically.

Take a moment sit still. Scan your body. Ask it:

- Where do I feel tight?
- What's heavy right now?
- What wants to be let go of?
- What am I carrying that isn't mine?

And then — here's the key — don't rush to fix it.

Just listen.

Let the feeling speak. Let the tension inform you. Let the fatigue say what it's been trying to say. Don't jump to productivity. Don't try to suppress it with positive thinking. Listen like you would to a child who finally feels safe enough to talk.

Because that's what your body is — it's the part of you that's held everything. All the stress. All the fear. All the decisions you made against your own truth.

And when you listen without judgment, the body starts to trust you again.

It starts to relax.
It starts to heal.
It starts to reveal truths the mind had buried.

This is how you rebuild the connection between mind and body — not by force, but by attention. By presence. By respect.

Your body is not your enemy.
It's not just a vessel to carry your brain.
It's not a problem to be fixed.
It's a living library. It remembers everything.
And it's been trying to talk to you this whole time.

Now that you've stopped, now that you've made space, it's your job to listen.

Because sometimes, the signal isn't a voice.

It's a knot in your stomach.

It's a tear you didn't expect.

It's an ache you've been ignoring for years.

That's the body saying: I've got something to tell you.

Listening to the Silence

Not everything that speaks uses words.
Not every truth has a voice.
Some of the most important things you will ever hear come wrapped in silence.

But silence unnerves us.

We've been trained to fill it — with music, with talking, with background noise, with scrolling, with anything but stillness. Silence feels threatening like something's missing. But that's only because we've forgotten what silence actually is.

Silence isn't emptiness.
Silence is space.
It's where clarity lives.
It's where wisdom breathes.
It's where the signal gets the volume it needs.

When you sit in silence long enough, you start to notice what's underneath the noise. Not just thoughts but patterns. Not just memories, but meaning. Emotions you've avoided rise to the surface. Desires you've silenced begin to whisper again. The pain you've numbed finally asks to be felt — and healed.

It's uncomfortable at first. The silence brings everything up.

This is why most people don't go there. They say they don't have time. They say they're too busy. But the truth is — they're afraid of what they'll hear when the distractions are gone. They're afraid of meeting themselves in the raw, unfiltered light of silence.

But if you want to heal, if you want to evolve, you have to go there.

Because silence is not a void — it's a mirror.

It reflects back everything that's real. Everything you've buried. Everything you've been trying to get back to. And once the panic passes, once the resistance softens, something miraculous happens:

You start to hear things you've never heard before.

- That quiet knowing: This is who I am.
- That flash of clarity: This is what I need to do next.
- That sacred presence: I'm not alone.

Silence is where the deeper self speaks.

It doesn't speak in language. It speaks in sense. In resonance. In presence. In alignment. You don't hear it with your ears — you feel it with your whole being, like a bell that rings inside your heart.

This is what people mean when they say "inner guidance."
It doesn't come with flashing lights.
It comes when the noise dies down enough for the truth to step forward.

So, sit in the silence. Don't rush it. Don't try to control it. Just let it open.

Let the quiet speak.
Let the truth rise.
Let the questions come without needing immediate answers.

Because sometimes, the deepest form of listening is saying:

"I'm here. I'm not running. I'm listening. I'm ready."

And that's when it speaks.

Rebuilding Trust with Yourself
Listening is more than hearing.
It's the foundation of trust.

Think about any relationship. When someone truly listens to you —
not just waiting to talk, not just nodding along, but listening — what
happens? You open up. You feel safe. You feel seen. You speak more
truth. You begin to trust.

Now, imagine what would change if you listened to yourself that
way.

Most people don't.

They override their own signals. They gaslight their instincts. They
betray their own intuition in exchange for approval, convenience, or
habit. They hear the warning signs and stay anyway. They feel the
resistance and push through. They ignore the "no" that rises up in
their gut and say "yes" to please.

And every time they do, they teach themselves this one dangerous
lesson:

"I can't be trusted."

But that's not the truth. You were born to know.
You were born to feel what's right, what's wrong, what's for you,
what's not.
The problem isn't that you don't know.
The problem is that you've stopped listening.

And without listening, there's no trust. Without trust, there's no
clarity.
And without clarity, your life becomes a maze — chasing answers
from everyone but yourself.

This is where the work begins. The healing work. The rebuilding.

It starts with small decisions. Micro-moments.

You feel tired, so you rest — even if your to-do list screams.
You feel dread, so you pause — even if the calendar says go.
You feel peace, so you lean in — even if it doesn't make "sense."
You hear your body say, "Not this," and you honor that.

And every time you do, something inside shifts.

You tell yourself, "I'm listening now."
And your whole system hears it.

That is the start of self-trust.

You stop second-guessing everything.
You stop needing external confirmation for internal truth.
You stop outsourcing your decisions to people who don't live your life.

You become your own compass.

This doesn't mean you never feel fear. It means you listen anyway.
It means you don't silence your inner voice because it's inconvenient or unpopular.
It means you're finally walking in alignment with your deepest knowing — and that changes everything.

When you listen to yourself, you come back into integrity.

Your body softens.
Your choices simplify.
Your clarity returns.

And most importantly, you remember:

The guidance you've been begging for has always been inside you.

It just needed your attention.

It needed your trust.

It needed you to stop long enough, get quiet enough, and listen long enough for it to speak.

Now you've heard it.

Now, the relationship begins again.

And from here, the real transformation starts.

Reflection: *The quite **voice** within isn't weak—**it is** your wisdom.*

REFLECT: *In this moment of stillness, let your thoughts **flow** onto the page.*

*- What **part** of me have been asking to be heard?*

REFLECT: *Listening to that **genuine nudge.***

*What voices have I **allowed** to speak over my own?*

REFLECT: *Give your **inner** voice space to speak.*

*What does my body say that my **mind** tries to silence?*

Mantra: *I **hear** with clarity as my **true** self—speaks **within** me.*

Sacred Pause

Breath—*I am alive.*

Presence—*I **am** here.*

Awareness—*Speak to me.*

Chapter Three: Learn

"He who learns but does not think is lost. He who thinks but does not learn is in great danger."

Confucius

Awareness Is the Door. Understanding Is the Key.
Awareness cracks the door open.
But it's understanding that walks you through.

Stopping gave you space.
Listening gave you insight.
But now — you need to learn from what you've seen.

Because awareness without understanding is just noise.
It's just, "I notice I'm doing it again."
"I keep choosing the wrong people."
"I keep numbing instead of feeling."
"I keep saying yes when I want to say no."

That's awareness — and it matters. It's where change begins.

But it's not the finish line.

If you don't take the next step — to understand what you're seeing — you'll stay trapped in a loop. Awake, but still repeating.
You'll be conscious but confused. Aware but frustrated.

And that's not freedom. That's just a more self-aware form of suffering.

So the question becomes:

What is this awareness trying to show me?

Not just "What am I doing?"
But: "Why do I keep doing it?"
"Where did I learn this?"
"What is this behavior protecting me from?"
"What does this part of me believe?"

Learning is about moving deeper.
It's about making meaning out of the messages your body, emotions, and patterns are sending you.

That recurring fear? It's not random.
That trigger? It's not irrational.
That resistance? It's trying to point you to something unresolved.

Learning asks you to slow down. To pause before you rush to fix. To let your awareness become understanding before you turn it into action.

Because if you skip this step, you'll just keep changing your behavior at the surface — while the root stays buried.

You don't just need new habits.
You need new meaning.

That's what learning is.

It's how you turn your awareness into wisdom.

And it starts by being willing to sit with what you've seen — long enough to ask, what is it saying to me?

Patterns Reveal Lessons

Life repeats itself until you pay attention. That's not punishment. That's being informed.

The same fight in a different relationship.
The same burnout in another job.
The same cycle with money, or trust, or your body, or your worth.
Different faces. Different settings. Same emotional spiral.

That's a pattern.
And it's not random.

Patterns are your personal curriculum.
They exist because something deep inside you is still unresolved —
and your system is looping through the same dynamics to try to
bring it to the surface.

Most people see a pattern and judge themselves:
"I can't believe I'm here again."
"I thought I was past this."
"I must not be growing."

But you are. You're just being asked to learn the deeper lesson this
time.

Because repetition is how life gets your attention.

When something keeps showing up, it's not because you're broken.
It's because something in you wants to be understood. Something
you didn't get as a child. Something you didn't have words for in the
past. Something that needs you to finally see it clearly.

That's the work:
- Noticing the pattern
- Sitting with the discomfort
- Asking what is this here to teach me?

Ask it:
- What do I keep expecting others to fix for me?
- What am I afraid will happen if I break this cycle?
- What part of me benefits from staying in this loop?

That last question is key.
Sometimes, your patterns are tied to safety. Familiarity. A role you played to survive. And to break them, you have to first understand what they gave you — even if it was dysfunctional.

Learning means honoring the function of your patterns without romanticizing the damage.

You get to say:
"I see why I did this. I see what it protected. I see what I was trying to get. And now that I understand, I can choose something better."

That's how the cycle ends.

Not by force.
Not by shame.
But by learning the lesson, the pattern came to teach.

Where Did I Learn This?
You weren't born with your patterns.

You weren't born self-doubting.
You weren't born afraid to rest, afraid to speak up, afraid to take up space.
You weren't born believing your worth depends on productivity, that love has to be earned, or that survival means silence.

You learned that.

And now, it's time to learn something new.

But before you can unlearn what's no longer serving you, you have to first understand where you learned it.

Because you didn't just wake up one day deciding to distrust your body, ignore your intuition, or abandon your boundaries.
That came from somewhere.

It came from a parent who only showed love when you achieved.
A culture that told you your value is in how much you produce.
A religion that confused obedience with wholeness.
A partner who rewarded self-sacrifice and punished truth.
A trauma that taught you the world is not safe — so you'd better stay small and stay alert.

Learning is about going back — not to relive, but to reveal.

- What story did I learn about being "good"?
- What belief did I inherit about success?
- What emotion was I told I wasn't allowed to feel?
- What did I normalize just to stay connected or safe?

This is shadow work.
Not to dwell in the past — but to understand the source.

Because here's what most people do:
They try to change the behavior without correcting the belief that drives it.
They try to set boundaries without releasing the guilt they were taught to feel.
They try to speak their truth without ever understanding why they learned to hide it.

But real learning means tracing the story to its root.
Because what was learned can be unlearned.

And what was internalized in pain can be re-written in truth.

So when you hear that inner voice say:

"You're not enough."
"This is your fault."
"Don't need too much. Don't feel too deep. Don't be too real."

Pause,
Ask yourself:

Whose voice is that?
And do I still believe it?
Or did I just forget to question it?

That's the beginning of freedom.
Not just changing the pattern — but changing the belief beneath it.

And from there, you begin to rewrite the story.

Not from blame.
But from clarity.

Not to stay stuck.
But to finally move forward.

Turn Pain into Perspective
Pain is a brutal teacher.
But it's also an honest one.

It shows up when something is off.
When something has been ignored, suppressed, denied, or avoided
for too long.
And if you let it — pain doesn't just hurt. It illuminates.

But most people never learn from their pain.
They just survive it.
They numb it.
They run from it.

They bury it so deep, they forget it ever happened — until it shows up again in the same pattern, different form.

Pain that isn't processed becomes recycled.

It leaks into your relationships.
It hardens into your worldview.
It turns into armor, mistrust, bitterness, and avoidance.

But here's the truth:

Pain holds wisdom — if you're willing to listen.

Not in the moment of impact — that's too raw.
But afterward. In the stillness. In the reflection.
When you stop asking, "Why me?" and start asking, "What did this wake up in me?"

That's where the perspective comes in.

You begin to ask:
- What was this pain trying to protect me from?
- What did it reveal about what I value?
- What part of me grew stronger because of this?
- What old belief system did this pain help me challenge or break?

This doesn't mean you glorify suffering.
It doesn't mean "everything happens for a reason."
It means you give your pain purpose.
You don't let it be wasted.

Learning from pain is not about moving on too fast.
It's about moving through — with your eyes open, your heart engaged, and your truth intact.

You don't become stronger by pretending it didn't happen.
You become stronger by saying:

"It happened. I felt it. I faced it. And now I know something I didn't know before."

And what you know now — that insight, that depth, that resilience — becomes part of your wisdom.

You can feel the difference in people who've learned from pain. They move slower. They listen better. They don't flinch at emotion. They carry presence. Weight. Clarity.

Because they didn't just survive what changed them.
They learned from it.

And in doing so, they turned pain into perspective — and perspective into power.

Integrating the Lesson
The lesson isn't complete until you carry it forward.

You can have the insight.
You can name the pattern.
You can understand the why.
But unless that wisdom begins to shape your next decision — it stays in the past.

Integration is what turns knowledge into guidance.
It's the moment you ask:
"Now that I know this — how do I move differently?"

Because learning doesn't end with understanding.
It begins when you start living the lesson.

You don't just say, "I deserve respect."
You stop engaging where it's denied.

You don't just say, "I need rest."
You actually structure your life to protect it.

You don't just say, "That belief came from fear."
You stop making decisions rooted in it.

This is how learning becomes leadership — not over others, but over yourself.

It's not dramatic. It's not loud. It's often invisible.

It looks like:

- Leaving when you used to stay
- Remaining when you used to give up
- Asking questions when you used to avoid them
- Holding space when you used to fill the silence with noise
- Honoring yourself when you used to outsource your value

The point isn't perfection. It's embodied intelligence.
You don't need to talk about the lesson anymore — because you've become the proof that you've learned it.

And sometimes? That lesson isn't even about what happened.
It's about how you carry yourself now.
How you treat others. How you protect your energy. How you lead with compassion but without betrayal.

Integration is subtle, but it's powerful.

It's when you stop needing the lesson to be fresh and start letting it be foundational.

You don't have to revisit the wound to remember the wisdom.
You just have to live it.

That's what makes the learning complete.

Reflection: *Learning is **remembering** what your **soul** never forgot.*

*What lesson **keeps** repeating itself in my life?*

REFLECT: *What have I been **taught** that I now question?*

REFLECT: *What quiet truth **within** me is still waiting to be **heard**?*

Pause: *for a moment to give it its voice. **Breath** will take you there.*

Mantra: What **I look** for is already **within-me.**

Sacred Pause

Breath— *I am **alive.***

Presence— *I am **here.***

Awareness— ***Speak** to me.*

Chapter Four: Apply

"Knowing is not enough; We must apply. Willing is not enough; we must do"

Johann Wolfgang von Goethe

Knowing Is Not Enough
You've stopped.
You've unplugged from the noise.
You've listened.
You've heard the truth inside you — maybe for the first time in years.

Now comes the part most people avoid: doing something with it.

We live in a time of information overload.
You can hear a hundred truths a day. Watch a thousand reels about healing. Read twenty books about purpose. Listen to five different podcasts about presence, power, or authenticity — and still live the exact same way.

Why?

Because knowing is not enough.

You can understand everything in theory and still be stuck in practice.
You can speak all the right language — alignment, self-love, intuition — and still betray yourself every day.

You can have breakthrough after breakthrough in your journal and still fall back into the same patterns in your life.

Information is not transformation.

Insight is the spark — but application is the fire.

Until you apply what you know, it doesn't belong to you.
It's just content.
It's potential.

Real transformation doesn't happen in your head. It happens in your habits. In your choices. In how you move through your day. In how you speak, how you rest, how you say yes and no, how you show up — not just when it's easy, but when it costs you something.

You say you want peace? Then you have to start choosing peace — not just admiring it.

You say you want alignment? Then, you have to stop saying yes to what drains you.

You say you want wholeness? Then, you have to stop betraying your body's signals to keep other people comfortable.

This is where the rubber meets the road.
This is where the spiritual gets practical.
This is where the listening turns into living.

It's not about perfection. It's about practice.

The question isn't: "Do you know what's true?"
The question is: "Are you living like you do?"

That's what application is.
It's the bridge between who you've been and who you're becoming.

And nobody can walk it for you.

Small Moves, Big Shifts
You don't need to change your whole life overnight.

In fact, if you try to, you'll probably burn out, crash, or slide back into old patterns. Real transformation doesn't happen through massive declarations or grand overhauls. It happens through small, consistent, courageous moves — repeated over time.

That's the work: not just realizing what needs to change but living it into existence one choice at a time.

You don't need to move to a new city. You don't need to quit your job tomorrow. You don't need to delete your social media and retreat into the mountains (unless that's the signal). What you do need to do is start living in alignment right now.

You know that truth you heard when you finally got quiet?

Start there.

If your body said "rest," go to bed earlier tonight.
If your soul said "leave," start planning your exit — even if it takes a year.
If your gut said, "This is not for you," stop pretending that it is.
If your truth said "speak," say the hard thing — even if you feel fear.

These are the real moves. The small ones. The honest ones. The ones nobody will clap for. The ones that seem invisible at first — but they are everything.

Because every time you act on your inner knowing, even in the smallest way, you send a message to your whole system: "I trust myself."

And every time you ignore it, dismiss it, or delay it — you reinforce the opposite.

71

So start with what's in front of you. That awkward conversation you've been avoiding. That boundary you keep collapsing. That lie you keep living because it's more convenient than the truth.

One small move. One shift. One honest action.

That's how new patterns begin.

That's how old identities start to fall apart.

That's how your life stops being something you manage — and starts becoming something you're actually living.

Remember: application isn't about changing everything at once.

It's about changing the direction.

And sometimes, turning one degree is all it takes to land in a different future.

Walking in Alignment
Alignment isn't an idea. It's a felt sense.

It's not a vibe. It's not aesthetic. It's not something you curate.
It's how your inner truth and outer life match — or don't.

You can feel it. When you're in alignment, your body relaxes. Your choices come with clarity. You don't second-guess every word. You sleep deeper. You breathe fuller. You speak more directly. You move with less friction and more flow. It's not always easy, but it feels right.

When you're out of alignment, everything feels heavier than it should.

You're tired, but not just physically — existentially.
You're dragging yourself through conversations that don't reflect your truth.

You say "yes" when you mean "no" and "it's fine" when it's not. You go places your spirit doesn't want to go. You fake your way through days.

That disconnect isn't random. It's your signal.

Your body's telling you: "This isn't the path."

But most of us were taught to override that voice — to perform, to please, to conform. We weren't raised to honor alignment. We were trained to seek approval.

So, walking in alignment takes unlearning.

It means listening to your body when it tenses — and getting curious.
It means noticing when you feel drained after being around certain people — and setting limits.
It means choosing what supports your truth — not just what's convenient or comfortable.

Alignment isn't about being fearless. It's about being honest.

It's saying, This relationship isn't healthy for me.
It's saying, This job looks good on paper but empties me inside.
It's saying, This version of me that everyone expects is not the full truth.
It's choosing truth over optics. Soul over strategy. Peace over performance.

And here's what's powerful:

The more you walk in alignment, the more momentum you build. Your body starts to trust you. Your intuition speaks louder. The right opportunities find you because you're no longer sending out a false signal.

People say alignment is "magnetic." It is — because it's real.

And real is rare.

When you move from alignment, your actions are not about proving anything.
They're about living in integrity with what you know to be true.
And that kind of life? It doesn't just feel better.
It works better.

You waste less energy.
You stop betraying yourself.
You stop attracting what isn't for you.

Because when you walk in alignment, life stops being a performance — and starts becoming yours.

Resistance, Sabotage, and Staying the Course

Let's be clear: the moment you start living your truth, resistance will show up.

Not if. When.

It's not a sign you're doing something wrong — it's proof that you're finally stepping out of the pattern.
And patterns don't break quietly.

Expect the friction. Expect the doubt. Expect the voice that says, "This is stupid. This won't last. Who do you think you are?"

That's your ego. That's your survival brain. That's the part of you that's been keeping you safe by keeping you small. And now you're threatening that safety by choosing growth. By applying what you've learned. By doing the uncomfortable thing that leads to freedom.

So, what does resistance look like?

Sometimes, it's obvious:
- Fear of what people will think
- Guilt when you set a boundary
- Overwhelm when you try to make a change
- A strong urge to go back to the familiar

But sometimes, it's subtle:
- You get "busy" and postpone that action you were committed to
- You start picking fights or making excuses
- You sabotage your own progress because the unknown feels scarier than the dysfunction you know

And here's what matters:

Don't confuse resistance with a red light.

Sometimes, resistance just means you're walking through a doorway. And the old self — the one that survived by playing small, staying silent, and keeping safe — is just fearful.

That part of you doesn't need punishment. It needs leadership.

So when resistance rises, don't run.
Don't numb. Don't collapse.
Lead yourself through it.

You say to that old voice:

"I hear you. I know you're scared. But we're not staying here."

This is what staying the course looks like.

It's not always glamorous. It's not always linear. It's messy. It's gritty. It takes courage to keep walking when the novelty wears off, and the discomfort kicks in. But that's when the work actually begins.

And here's what no one tells you:
Your breakthrough often hides behind the resistance.
The freedom you want lives on the other side of that "I can't do this" moment.
And if you can just stay with it — not perfectly, but honestly — you'll make it through.

Every time you move through resistance without abandoning yourself, you strengthen the muscle of self-trust.
Every time you stay the course instead of self-sabotaging, you teach your nervous system that change is survivable.
And eventually, application becomes easier. Not because life gets easier — but because you get stronger.

This isn't about forcing your way through.
It's about showing up when it matters.
It's about walking your truth even when you don't feel like it.

That's how you change a life.

One hard choice at a time.

Embodied Truth
You'll know you've applied the truth when you no longer have to think about it.

You just live it.

It's no longer something you're trying to remember, trying to force, trying to recite like a mantra.
It's in your posture. Your pace. Your decisions.
It's in how you speak, how you rest, how you hold a boundary, how you say no with love and yes without apology.

It's no longer theory. It's embodied.

This is the moment when people say, "You're different."
Not louder. Not more polished. Not more "together."
Just real. Rooted. Clear. Quietly powerful.

Because your energy no longer comes from performance.
It comes from alignment.

You don't chase peace — you walk in it.
You don't fight for clarity — it follows you.
You don't seek validation — because you've already validated
yourself through action.

That's embodied truth.

It's in the deep breath you take instead of reacting.

It's in the seven minutes of stillness you protect every morning — no
matter what.

It's in the choice to walk away from what no longer matches who
you've become, even when it costs you comfort.

It's not loud. It's not flashy. But it's unmistakable.

And here's the part most people miss:

Embodiment isn't perfection.
It's consistency.

It's not getting it right every day. It's returning to the truth faster.
It's noticing when you're off-track and coming back — not with
shame, but with presence.

You apply, you adjust, you evolve.
You keep walking. You keep choosing.
Until one day, you look up and realize — this isn't something you're
practicing anymore.

This is just who you are now.

The signal is no longer something you're trying to hear.
You've become the signal.

And from here, you don't just live the truth — you radiate it.

You become the permission someone else has been waiting for.

You become the example your past self needed.

You become the one who stopped, who listened, who applied — and who became whole.

And that's where we go next.

Reflection: *Wisdom only lives when it **walks**, what it **talks**.*

REFLECT: *Where have I **delayed** action out of fear?*

REFLECT: *What is one small **action** I can take that aligns with what I know?*

REFLECT: *What am I **ready** to embody today?*

Mantra: *I move from **knowing** to living.*

Sacred Pause

Breath—*I am alive.*

Presence— *I **am** here.*

Awareness—*Speak to me.*

Chapter Five: Develop

"Excellence is an art won by training and habituation."

Aristotle

Practice Builds Power
You've listened. You've applied.
Now comes the part most people skip: practice.

This is where transformation becomes real.

Because applying the truth once? That's a spark.
But repeating it? That's how you build fire.

Power isn't found in big breakthroughs — it's built through small, consistent practice. Over time. Especially when no one's watching. Especially when it's not exciting anymore. Especially when everything in you wants to default to the old way.

That's what development is: choosing to stay in alignment long enough for it to become natural.

You don't build muscle by lifting a weight once.
You don't become a strong communicator by having one honest conversation.
You don't rewrite your nervous system with a single meditation.

It takes reps.
It takes rhythm.
It takes commitment to the process after the hype wears off.

This is where many people fall off. They think transformation is supposed to feel electric all the time. They expect every step to feel like a breakthrough. But here's the truth:

Practice is often boring. But it's never wasted.

Every time you choose integrity, when it would be easier to shrink. That's-Power.
Every time you slow down and breathe instead of reacting? Power.
Every time you return to yourself after slipping into old habits — without shame, without quitting, Power.

That's how you grow capacity.

You're building a new normal. A new way of being. And that takes more than insight. It takes integration.

The first time you say no, it feels terrifying.
The fifth time, it feels strong.
The fiftieth time, it feels normal.

That's what repetition does. It rewires your reflexes.

And one day, what used to take everything in you to pull off becomes second nature.
Not because you're forcing it — but because you've developed into someone who doesn't need to fake it anymore.

This is your power now.
Not because you read it.
Not because you posted about it.
But because you lived it. Again and again.

Power is earned through practice.
And practice, over time, makes the truth unshakable.

Growth Under Pressure
Everything you're developing will get tested.

Not to punish you.
To refine you.

The real world doesn't care how self-aware you are when everything is calm. The real world wants to know: Can you stay grounded when it's not?
Can you hold your alignment when life pushes back?
Can you stay true to yourself under the pressure of real relationships, deadlines, triggers, and disappointments?

That's where development lives — in the tension.

Because anyone can meditate in silence.
Anyone can be kind when they feel good.
Anyone can speak the truth when the stakes are low.
But can you do it under pressure?
Can you do it when you're tired, when you're afraid, when you're doubting everything?

That's the difference between performance and embodiment.

Growth isn't clean. It's not polished. It's not a perfect arc. It's usually messy, emotional, uncertain. You'll slip. You'll regress. You'll say, "I thought I was past this." But you're not back at square one — you're in the lab.

The pressure isn't a sign you're failing.
It's an invitation to deepen.

That moment, you catch yourself mid-pattern and pause instead of reacting?
That's development.

That moment you speak up — not perfectly, but honestly,
That's development.

That moment you feel the urge to self-sabotage, and instead, you just sit with it.
That's development.

You're building durability.
You're proving to yourself that you can hold the truth you've found — not just in ideal conditions, but in real life.

Pressure doesn't kill growth.
It reveals it.

And if you meet that pressure with presence — not perfection — you'll come out stronger every time.

You don't have to pass every test. You just have to stay in the process.

Because over time, you stop getting thrown by every wave.
You stop doubting yourself the second things get hard.
You stop abandoning your truth when it's inconvenient.

You develop roots.

And once something's rooted, it doesn't just survive storms.

It thrives through them.

Self-Awareness Is a Skill
Self-awareness isn't a trait you either have or don't.

It's a skill.
And like any skill, it can be developed — with practice, patience, and intention.

When you first begin to wake up, your awareness feels raw and overwhelming. You notice things you didn't want to see. Patterns. Reactions. The way you shrink. The lies you tell. The tension you carry. The energy you ignore. It can be a lot.

But the longer you stay with it, the more skilled you become at noticing without spiraling.

You start to recognize your triggers faster.
You notice the stories you're telling yourself — in real-time.
You feel when your energy shifts. You catch when your body tightens.
You see the pattern as it's happening — not just after it's wrecked your day.

That's development.

You no longer live on autopilot. You observe. You witness. You choose.

And here's the shift: self-awareness stops being just about self-criticism — and becomes a tool for self-leadership.

You no longer say, "Ugh, why am I like this?"

You say, "Ah — there it is. I see it. And I know what to do now."

You stop labeling yourself. You start listening to yourself.
You stop reacting to pain. You start responding from presence.

That's a developed self-awareness:
- Less drama.
- More discernment.

- Less shame.
- More responsibility.
- Less perfectionism.
- More compassion.

You realize: I don't need to be flawless. I just need to be awake.

And the more awake you become, the more power you have to redirect — not because you're fighting yourself, but because you understand yourself.

It's not about controlling every reaction.

It's about catching yourself sooner, choosing better faster, and recovering with grace when you don't.

That's mastery.

Not control.
Not image.
But an honest, lived-in, moment-to-moment relationship with your truth.

And that kind of awareness?

That changes everything.

Integration Over Time
This work isn't quick.

It's not flashy. It's not linear. It's not something you can rush or, hack or binge your way through.
Real development takes time.

Not just time passing — but time spent showing up.

You are here to build a moment by moment that builds a life. That kind of foundation doesn't happen overnight. It happens through integration.

Integration means:
- The truth doesn't just live in your head — it lives in your habits.
- The shifts don't just happen when you feel inspired — they show up when you're tired, stressed, triggered, or tempted.
- Your growth doesn't just show when you post — it shows when no one's watching.

It's the long game.

And this is where many people lose focus. They want transformation to feel dramatic every day. They want big wins and constant breakthroughs. But the most meaningful growth often feels... quiet.

It's when you go to bed a little earlier — again.
It's when you say no to chaos — again.
It's when you hold a boundary — again.
It's when you notice your trigger and breathe — again.

That's integration.

It's the shift from: "How do I fix this right now?"
To: "How do I live this consistently for the rest of my life?"

It's not just about intensity. It's about rhythm.
It's not about doing the work for a week. It's about becoming the work overtime.

That's what makes this sustainable.

Because anyone can change their behavior for a month.
But integration is about becoming someone true — from the inside out — through repetition, reflection, and real-world practice.

And over time, you realize:

- You don't get triggered the way you used to.
- You bounce back faster.
- You're less reactive, more grounded.
- You're not chasing peace — you live it.
- You're not gripping for clarity — it's woven into your pace, your posture, your presence.

This is how you build depth.

This is how you build resilience.

This is how you build a life that doesn't need to be constantly restructured — because it's already aligned.

And yeah — it takes time.

But if you're in this for real change, for real freedom, for a life that actually feels like yours — you don't need fast.

You need true.

And true takes time.

Rooted and Ready
You have done the work. You've stopped running. You've listened.
You've applied the truth.
You've practiced it when it was uncomfortable.
You've stayed with it when it was boring.
You've grown through the pressure.
You've deepened your awareness.
You've integrated it over time.

Now — you're not just aware.
You're not just in motion.

You're rooted.

And here's what that feels like:

- You don't chase clarity — because you are clear.
- You don't fake confidence — because it's embodied.
- You don't need constant validation — because you trust yourself.
- You don't fear disruption — because your peace doesn't depend on things staying perfect.

You're grounded — not because life got easier, but because you got stronger.

You're not easily pulled off course anymore.
You don't panic when plans change.
You don't shrink when people disapprove.
You don't break every time a wave hits.

You bend.
You adapt.
You hold center.

Because your foundation isn't built on performance anymore — it's built on presence.

And when you're rooted, you're finally ready.

Ready to show up more fully.
Ready to serve from overflow, not exhaustion.
Ready to lead without losing yourself.
Ready to receive without guilt.
Ready to face what comes next — not with force, but with steadiness.

This is not the end of your growth.
This is the beginning of your strength.

You're not here to stay in development forever. You're here to live what you've built.
To move from it. To expand from it. To help others find their way — because you've walked the path.

You don't have all the answers. You don't need to.
You have your roots.
You have your rhythm.
You have your truth — lived, tested, refined.

And that?

That makes you ready.

Reflection: *Growth isn't about gaining — it's about **maturing**.*

REFLECT: *What is quietly **unfolding** within me?*

REFLECT: *What brings me **back** to myself when **I** feel unsteady?*

REFLECT: *What part of **me** is quietly evolving beneath the surface?*

*Take a moment to **listen**.*

Mantra: *Even in **silence**, I am maturing.*

Sacred Pause

Breath— *I am **alive.***

Presence— *I am **here**.*

Awareness— *Speak to **me**.*

Chapter Six: Become

"The privilege of a lifetime is to become who you truly are."
Carl Jung

Becoming Isn't Something You Chase
You don't become by chasing.
You don't become by forcing.
You don't become by performing, hustling, or striving to reach some final version of yourself.

Becoming isn't a destination.
It's a state.
A frequency.
A deep, quiet alignment with who you already are — without the noise, without the mask, without the distortion.

You don't become by adding more.
You become by letting go of what's not you.

This is what most people get wrong.

They think becoming is about fixing. Leveling up. Adding skills. Changing their personality. Getting more knowledge, more status, more discipline, more validation.

But real becoming?

It's not about adding. It's about uncovering.

The truth is already there — buried beneath layers of fear, programming, shame, and expectations.

And the journey you've taken — to stop, to listen, to learn, to apply, to develop — wasn't about turning into someone else.

It was about removing everything that wasn't real.

And now? What's left is you.

Not the curated version. Not the one designed to be liked.
Not the version shaped by fear of rejection.
Not the version of surviving in a world that never saw you clearly.

The real you. The rooted you. The aligned you.

And this version of you?

You don't chase her.
You don't perform for him.
You don't beg for it.

You let it emerge.

It shows up in how you move and how you speak, how you breathe, how you choose.

It's not something you arrive at with fanfare.
It's something you wake up one day and realize you've been walking in all along.

This is what becoming feels like:

- It's quiet.
- It's clear.
- It doesn't need to be announced.
- It doesn't need to be proven.
- It's simply true.

You're not chasing your best self anymore.

You're simply being the most honest version of yourself.

And that changes everything.

What Falls Away When You Become
Becoming isn't just about what you gain.
It's about what you shed.

Because when you start living from the truth — fully,
unapologetically — you don't just grow into yourself.
You let go of everything that kept you out of alignment.

Old identities.
Outdated roles.
Social masks.
False obligations.
The version of you that was built to survive instead of thrive.

These pieces don't fall off all at once.
They start to crumble. They fade. They resist.
Sometimes, they go down swinging.

But you know you're becoming when certain things just stop making
sense:

- Performing for approval
- Apologizing for your energy
- Staying small to make others comfortable
- Holding on to relationships just to prove you're loyal
- Saying yes to what you've outgrown

You lose the urge to explain.
You stop negotiating your worth.
You stop playing roles you never chose.

And yes — sometimes that's terrifying.
Because parts of you have been built around those roles.
You were "the responsible one," "the fixer," "the achiever," "the peacemaker," "the strong one."
And letting go of those identities can feel like dying — because, in a way, it is.

But what dies isn't you.

What dies is the version of you that was built on fear.

And when it falls away?
There's space.

Space to breathe.
Space to speak.
Space to trust yourself.
Space to just be.

This is where wholeness begins.

Not in becoming more, but in finally living less divided.

One self. One voice. One presence.

That's what becoming gives you.

Not a new mask — but your actual face.

Not a better script — but your true voice.

And as the false identities fall away, what's left is the most powerful, magnetic, grounded thing in the world:

You, as you are.

You Are Who You Practice Being

Becoming isn't a moment.
It's a pattern.

You don't just become someone new because you had a
breakthrough or made a big decision.
You become someone new because you practice it.
Over and over.
Until it stops feeling like practice — and starts feeling like you.

This is one of the most liberating truths in life:

You are not defined by your past.
You are shaped by your present choices.

If you keep acting like the old version of you — the version who said
yes to everything, who didn't speak up, who stayed quiet, who
moved from fear — then you'll stay aligned with that identity.

But the moment you begin to move differently —
- To choose boundaries over burnout
- To speak your truth even when it's not accepted
- To honor your energy instead of managing perception
- To sit with discomfort instead of escaping it

—you're telling your nervous system, your subconscious, and your
future:
"This is who I am now."

You are what you repeat.

And repetition is how you train the body, the mind, and the soul to
trust the new frequency you're living in.

It's not about doing it perfectly.
It's about doing it consistently enough to become familiar.
Because what's familiar is what feels like "you."

So ask yourself:

- What version of me am I rehearsing right now?
- What identity am I reinforcing through my daily choices?
- Is this who I want to become — or who I've been conditioned to be?

Becoming happens when you start acting in alignment with your truth — before it feels natural.

You practice the person you're becoming until it becomes your baseline.

You don't fake it — you retrain it.

You walk the walk.

You stop needing constant motivation — because you've made integrity your default.

And that's how the new identity clicks into place:

Not from thinking.
From living.

You aren't who you say you are.
You are who you consistently choose to be.

Becoming Means Belonging to Yourself
This is the turning point.

You've stopped betraying yourself for belonging.
You've stopped twisting your truth to fit in.
You've stopped shrinking to stay safe.

Because real becoming means this:

You finally belong to yourself.

You don't just know who you are — you honor it.
You stay with it.
You protect it.
You refuse to abandon it, even when it's inconvenient, even when it costs you relationships, approval, or comfort.

That's the shift.

You no longer shape yourself to match the room — you choose the rooms where you don't have to.

You no longer wait to be chosen — because you've already chosen yourself.

This is the end of code-switching, people-pleasing, and walking on emotional eggshells.
You stop editing your truth to be digestible.
You stop making yourself smaller to stay likable.

You realize:
If I have to lose myself to be accepted, it's not acceptance — it's abandonment.

And you've done enough of that.

Now, the relationship you're most committed to is the one inside — between you and your inner world.
Between your truth and your actions.
Between your soul and your structure.

This kind of inner belonging changes everything:

- You stop asking for permission.
- You stop craving external validation.
- You stop outsourcing your identity to people who don't even know themselves.

You walk into rooms with nothing to prove.

You listen to your own yes and your own no.

You stop apologizing for your clarity, your peace, your strength, your presence.

And that's when you finally feel home.

Not because the world made space for you —
But because you made space for yourself.

This is what freedom feels like:
Belonging within.
Belonging without conditions.
Belonging that starts in your heart — and radiates out in everything you do.

This Is Just the Beginning
Becoming isn't an end.
It's an opening.

You didn't come this far just to arrive.
You came this far to finally begin — as yourself.

The false starts, the self-abandonment, the survival mode, the loops — those were all chapters in a story that needed to be lived so you could write a new one.

And now, for the first time, you're writing it on your terms.

You're not waking up and reacting to life.
You're waking up and responding — from your truth, your alignment, your wholeness.

You're not chasing meaning anymore.
You're making it — with every boundary, every breath, every move that honors who you really are.

And here's what's beautiful:

You're not finished.
You're just rooted.

And from this root, you can grow anywhere.

- You can expand without losing yourself.
- You can lead without performing.
- You can serve without burning out.
- You can evolve without erasing what matters.

Because you're not becoming something new.
You're becoming someone true.

And from this place of truth — anything is possible.

You don't need a five-year plan.
You need a clear compass.
And now you have one: you.

You've stopped.
You've listened.
You've learned.
You've applied.
You've developed.
You've become.

And now?

You live it.

This is not the end of the journey—This is the beginning—Everyday is a new day to appreciate the moment of awareness.

Reflection: *"Becoming isn't arriving. It's **returning.**"*

REFLECT: *I have **found** what I have been **looking** for.*

REFLECT: *It feels good to be me.*

REFLECT: *I am **enough.***

Sacred Pause

Breath— *I am* **here.**

Presence— *Is my* **home.**

Awareness— *has* **led** *me out of the* **darkness** *and into the* **light.**

Closing Thoughts

This journey of sacred stopping has been about exactly that. Stopping to feel. Listening to hear. Learning to trust. Applying with love. Developing with humility. Becoming with courage.

You don't need to change into someone else. You just need to remember who you already are.

And when you forget — return. That's the power of awareness. That's the gift of being alive.

As you walk forward — into your days, your seasons, your years — I leave you with this:

I wish you peace.

I wish you clarity.

I wish you the kind of freedom that comes not from escaping the noise, but from remembering the signal beneath it.

Art Tincher

Note to the Reader

The words in this book are more than language — they are tools.

Some carry meanings you may already know. Others are used in ways that reflect a deeper, lived experience.

This glossary is here to offer clarity, not just definitions. It's here to help you understand the frequency behind the words — the intention, the presence, the practice.

Let these entries serve as a guide as you move through your own process of stopping, listening, learning, applying, developing, and becoming.

Come back to them whenever you need grounding. The meaning isn't just in the words — it's in how you live them.

Glossary Terms – Chapter 1

Stillness

More than the absence of movement or noise — stillness is the presence of truth. It is a conscious state of being where the mind quiets, the body settles, and awareness rises. Stillness is where intelligence, insights, and alignment is. It is not weakness. It is sacred space.

Stopping

A radical act of reclaiming power. Stopping means unplugging from external stimulation, silencing distractions, and turning inward. It's not just resting — it's intentionally ceasing all motion to become present with what is. It's how we return to ourselves.

Sacred

Not a religious term in this context, but a recognition of something deeply valuable, essential, and life-giving. "Sacred" points to pure moments, spaces, or truths that reconnect us to what matters. It's the felt sense that something is worthy of reverence — including your own breath, awareness, and existence.

Psychic Fragmentation

The internal disconnection that occurs when the self is split by constant distraction, over-stimulation, and busyness. It shows up as emotional numbness, identity confusion, or feeling scattered and lost. Awareness begins when we become still enough to notice — and reintegrate.

The Machine

A metaphor for the external systems — social, technological, economic — that feed on your attention, energy, and productivity. The machine thrives on your distraction and exhaustion. It resists stillness because it loses power when you reclaim your presence.

Survival Mode

A reactive state of being where the nervous system is stuck in alertness. In survival mode, decisions are made from fear, anxiety, or overwhelm. True presence and peace are inaccessible until the body and mind are allowed to rest and reset.

Dopamine

A chemical messenger in the brain that plays a major role in reward, motivation, and pleasure. The constant stimulation of screens and notifications triggers dopamine spikes, creating addiction-like patterns. Awareness helps us shift from dopamine-chasing to meaningful living.

Nervous System

The body's communication network, connecting brain and body. It regulates how we respond to stress, rest, and everything in between. In this work, we bring attention to calming the nervous system — moving from high-alert states into grounded presence and clarity.

Unified Field (of Consciousness)

A state of wholeness where awareness is undivided — beyond thought, beyond ego, beyond separation. It's the space of direct connection to life, to being, and to truth. It is not a belief, but an experience — often felt in deep stillness, pure—presence, or silence. Zero-Point Field.

Subconscious Programming

The unseen patterns, beliefs, and behaviors formed by societal conditioning, past experiences, and repeated exposure to stimulation. These programs run beneath conscious awareness and drive many of our reactions — especially around productivity and worth.

Presence

Being fully here — in this moment, in this body, in this breath. Presence is undivided attention. It is when your mind, body, and spirit are aligned in awareness. Presence heals fragmentation and reconnects you to what matters most.

Mantra

A spoken or silent phrase used as a tool of focus and intention. In this work, a mantra is not used for ritual or religion — it's a conscious reminder that re-centers the self in presence.

Example: "In stopping, I return, back to the true me."

Sacred Pause

An intentional break from movement, noise, or reaction — where you allow breath, presence, and awareness to recalibrate your system. The sacred pause is where clarity begins and energy is restored. It's not wasted time. It's the foundation of conscious living.

Wholeness

The natural state of your being when you are not fragmented, distracted, or performing. Wholeness isn't something you earn — it's something you remember. It lives beneath the noise, and it can only be accessed through stillness and self-awareness.

Glossary Terms – Chapter Two

Noise

Mental clutter, external influence, or internal programming that distorts truth and creates distraction. Noise speaks with urgency, fear, judgment, and repetition. It keeps you in loops of reaction, not clarity.

Signal

The quiet voice of God, intuition, and inner wisdom. Signal doesn't compete for attention. It's calm, grounded, and aligned with your deeper self. You must turn down the noise to hear it.

Inner Guidance

The non-verbal knowing that rises from within — your intuition, your body, your inner truth. Inner guidance is accessed through silence and self-trust, not logic or outside approval.

Embodied Listening

The act of tuning in not only with your mind, but with your body, your breath, and your felt sense. It's listening to what your body is experiencing, signaling, or asking for without judgment or rush.

Body Intelligence

The inner wisdom of the body — expressed through sensations, tension, relaxation, or physical responses. It communicates clearly when something is aligned or misaligned, often before the mind knows.

Conditioned Voice

A repeated internal narrative that originates from past programming, societal expectations, trauma, or authority figures. Often mistaken for intuition, this voice tends to speak in fear, guilt, or self-judgment.

Listening

More than hearing — listening in this work means receiving with presence, pure—openness, and curiosity. It is how we rebuild trust, find alignment, and reawaken clarity.

Silence

Not the absence of sound, but the presence of spaciousness. Silence is a mirror that reflects truth. It's the ground where clarity, connection, and inner wisdom are revealed.

Self-Trust

The confidence that your inner guidance is valid and trustworthy. Self-trust grows when you consistently listen to, honor, and act on what you feel to be true within yourself.

Alignment

A state of congruence between your inner truth and your outer actions. Living in alignment means choosing what resonates deeply, even when it's inconvenient or misunderstood by others.

Glossary Terms – Chapter Three

Awareness

The initial recognition or noticing of thoughts, feelings, or behaviors. It opens the door to change but must be followed by understanding and integration to create real transformation.

Understanding

The deeper interpretation of what awareness reveals. It helps you connect patterns to their roots, turning insight into meaning and meaning into wisdom.

Patterns

Repeated emotional, mental, or behavioral loops that reveal underlying beliefs or unresolved experiences. Patterns are your personal curriculum — not punishments, but invitations to learn.

Shadow Work

The process of exploring unconscious beliefs, hidden fears, and parts of yourself that were shaped by early conditioning or pain. It helps bring buried truth into the light.

Unlearning

The conscious process of releasing beliefs, habits, and narratives that were adopted through conditioning but no longer serve your growth or truth.

Integration

The final step of true learning. It means allowing the wisdom you've gained to shape your decisions, boundaries, habits, and way of being — until the lesson becomes part of your foundation.

Embodied Intelligence

Wisdom that's not just understood intellectually but felt, lived, and expressed through your actions. It's the proof that you've not only learned something but become it.

Conditioning

The beliefs and behaviors you absorbed from family, culture, religion, or experience that shaped your inner world. Much of what you call 'truth' may simply be conditioning that can be re-examined.

Pain as Teacher

The idea that pain, when honored and processed, carries important messages about boundaries, values, Identity, and self-worth. It can become a source of perspective and transformation.

Curriculum of the Soul

The deeper life lessons each person is here to face and grow through. These often show up in recurring patterns, difficult relationships, or repeated challenges — all designed for awakening and growth.

Glossary Terms – Chapter Four

Application

The act of putting inner wisdom into practice through aligned action. Application bridges the gap between what you know and how you live.

Embodied Truth

Truth that has been fully integrated into how you live, speak, move, and choose. It's no longer something you remind yourself of — it's how you operate.

Information vs. Transformation

Information is knowledge acquired through content; transformation is the result of living that knowledge consistently. Knowing something is not enough — doing something with it changes you.

Resistance

The mental, emotional, or physical friction that arises when you begin to change. Often mistaken for a sign to stop, resistance can be a natural response from the ego or survival brain to unfamiliar growth.

Self-Sabotage

Behaviors or thought patterns that unconsciously block your own growth or success. Often rooted in fear, guilt, or internalized beliefs that resist change or freedom.

Walking in Alignment

Living in a way that matches your inner truth. It shows up in your daily actions, boundaries, decisions, and energy. Alignment isn't a feeling — it's a way of being.

Small Moves

The subtle, consistent choices that create real transformation. These include setting boundaries, resting when needed, or telling the truth — even when it's inconvenient or uncomfortable.

Performance vs. Presence

Performance is living for approval, looking good, or staying safe through appearance. Presence is living from truth, groundedness, and authenticity, regardless of outcome.

Staying the Course

The practice of continuing forward through discomfort, fear, or uncertainty. It means honoring the path even when it's hard — and building strength through consistency.

The Signal

In this chapter, it evolves from something you listen to into something you become. The signal is your embodied wisdom, inner guidance, and integrated truth made visible.

Glossary Terms – Chapter Five

Practice

The ongoing repetition of aligned actions and decisions. Practice builds strength, reinforces change, and transforms insight into instinct. It's where theory becomes muscle.

Development

The phase where growth deepens through repetition, pressure, and real-life integration. It's not about new information but living known truths consistently.

Integration

The process of internalizing what you've learned so that it becomes a natural part of how you live, choose, and respond — not occasionally, but consistently over time.

Self-Awareness

A skill that grows through practice. It's your ability to observe your thoughts, patterns, triggers, and energy in real time — and respond with clarity instead of reaction.

Growth Under Pressure

The testing ground for transformation. True growth isn't proven in calm — it's revealed in challenge, conflict, and discomfort. Pressure reveals how much you've developed.

Durability

The ability to stay rooted in your truth even under stress, discomfort, or temptation to regress. Durability is built through repeated practice and deepened awareness.

Embodiment

When truth becomes how you live, not just what you believe. Embodiment is shown in actions, choices, and posture — not just words. It's the lived evidence of transformation.

Rootedness

A grounded inner state that remains steady regardless of external chaos. When you're rooted, you move from presence, not performance, and respond instead of reacting.

Resilience

The capacity to return to center after disruption. It's not about avoiding difficulty — it's about becoming someone who can meet difficulty without losing alignment.

Long Game

The mindset that values sustainable change over quick fixes. It's the commitment to depth, rhythm, and integration — knowing that real transformation takes time.

Glossary Terms – Chapter Six

Becoming

Not a destination but a process of uncovering the truth of who you already are. Becoming is about releasing what's false, not adding more. It is the emergence of your most honest, aligned self.

Uncovering

The process of letting go of fear, programming, and roles that do not reflect your true self. Uncovering allows your authentic identity to come forward naturally.

Identity

Not a fixed label but a fluid experience shaped by practice, alignment, and choice. You are who you consistently choose to be — not who you've been conditioned to be.

Belonging to Yourself

The act of honoring, trusting, and choosing your own truth over external approval. It's the end of self-abandonment and the beginning of inner alignment.

Practiced Self

The version of you that becomes real through repeated, embodied choices. You become who you practice being — with every decision, boundary, and breath.

Internal Compass

Your inner guidance system. It's the clarity, alignment, and integrity that guide your choices from within — without relying on outside permission or validation.

Self-Abandonment

The act of ignoring or overriding your truth to gain acceptance or avoid discomfort. Growth begins when you stop betraying yourself and choose to belong inwardly.

Rootedness (in Becoming)

A state of inner stability and wholeness. It means you're no longer seeking clarity or worth from outside — you live from it, and it informs how you move, speak, and choose.

Frequency

The energetic state or felt vibration of your truth. Becoming aligns you with your natural frequency — your authentic presence beyond performance or pretense.

The Beginning

Becoming is not the end of growth — it is the beginning of true living. From this rooted place, expansion, contribution, and deeper connection become possible.

Sources of Influence

Tony Robbins — *Awaken the Giant Within*

Robbins explores how identity, emotions, and beliefs shape action and outcomes. He emphasizes the importance of raising personal standards, making conscious decisions, and using tools like Neuro-Associative Conditioning (NAC) to create lasting change. At the heart of his message is the call to embrace growth as a lifelong commitment.

Daniel Kahneman — *Thinking, Fast and Slow*

Kahneman introduces two systems of thought — one fast and intuitive, the other slow and analytical. His work reveals how awareness of these systems can lead to better decision-making, helping individuals respond with greater clarity rather than reacting automatically.

Jack Canfield — *The Success Principles*

Canfield stresses the power of clarity — knowing where you are, where you want to go, and what needs to change. A core teaching, E + R = O (Event + Response = Outcome), highlights the importance of taking full responsibility and choosing conscious responses to life's challenges.

Eckhart Tolle — *A New Earth*

This book invites readers to let go of labels, judgments, and the constant need to define everything. Tolle teaches the power of being fully present — even in the simplest moments, like washing your hands or observing the breath. His message points to a deeper awareness that exists beneath thought, where stillness and clarity reside.

Dr. Wayne Dyer — *Excuses Begone! *

Dyer challenges the patterns of excuse-making and encourages a mindset rooted in personal responsibility and forward movement. His message centers on replacing limiting thoughts with empowering ones and shifting from blame to ownership. The work promotes inner freedom through conscious thinking and a positive, purpose-driven perspective.

Thich Nhat Hanh — *The Art of Living*

This work offers a gentle invitation to practice deep listening — creating space for others to share their pain without interruption, judgment, or the need to fix. With presence and compassion, true healing begins. The teaching emphasizes that listening with empathy can ease suffering and restore peace, both within and between people.

Nancy Colier — *Can't Stop Thinking*

This book brings clarity to the nature of thought, showing that thoughts are not the self — they are events passing through awareness. Colier emphasizes the power of mindfulness and meditation to create space between observer and thought. By witnessing the mind rather than identifying with it, freedom and inner stillness become accessible.

Greg Epstein — *Good Without God*

Epstein presents a humanistic perspective that goodness does not require belief in a higher power or expectation of reward. Ethical living is shown to be a conscious choice — grounded in compassion, responsibility, and integrity. The act of doing good becomes its own reward, rooted in values rather than external validation.

Jon Kabat-Zinn — *Mindfulness for Beginners*

Kabat-Zinn presents mindfulness as a natural human ability to be present with life as it is — moment by moment, without judgment. His approach removes religious or mystical framing and emphasizes mindfulness as a secular, practical, and universal tool for self-awareness, healing, and living more fully. The practice of meditation is shown not as exclusive to any culture, but as a timeless human capacity — rooted in introspection, imagination, and direct experience long before it was given a name.

Johann Hari — *Stolen Focus*

Hari explores the modern crisis of attention, revealing how technology, media, and environmental factors are constantly pulling focus away from the present moment. His work emphasizes the importance of reclaiming attention through intentional choices — such as limiting distractions, slowing down, and being fully engaged with everyday experiences. The message is clear: presence is not only possible, but essential for a meaningful life.

Dr. Anna Lembke — *Dopamine Nation*

Lembke examines the modern addiction to pleasure and distraction, showing how the constant pursuit of dopamine often masks unresolved pain. Her work encourages facing discomfort rather than sedating it — revealing that when pain is embraced with honesty and space, it often dissolves. Through balance, discipline, and awareness, healing becomes possible without escape.

Dr. Steven Novella — *Your Deceptive Mind*

Novella explores the nature of human cognition and the many ways the mind can deceive itself through bias, faulty logic, and illusion. His work offers tools for critical thinking — teaching how to distinguish fact from fiction, question assumptions, and embrace empirical evidence. It aligns closely with mindfulness, inviting a deeper awareness of how the mind works and the importance of seeing things as they truly are.

Continue the Journey

If something in these pages spoke to you, you're invited to go deeper. Visit: apuremoment.com

 This is more than a book — it's the beginning of a new relationship with yourself and creating a lasting change. You don't have to do it alone. I'm here to help you move forward with clarity, structure, and accountability — so you can get where you want to go, without wasting time.

Art Tincher

www.ingramcontent.com/pod-product-compliance
Lightning Source LLC
Chambersburg PA
CBHW051207120626
46547CB00013B/1238